GUIDELINES O
Instruments Of The Orchestra

by Lee Ching Ching

© RHYTHM MP SDN. BHD. 1996

Published by
RHYTHM MP SDN. BHD.
1947, Lorong IKS Bukit Minyak 2,
Taman IKS Bukit Minyak, 14100 Simpang Ampat,
Penang, Malaysia.
Tel: +60 4 5050246 (Direct Line), +60 4 5073690 (Hunting Line)
Fax: +60 4 5050691
E-mail: rhythmmp@mphsb.com
Website: www.rhythmmp.com

Perpustakaan Negara Malaysia Cataloguing-in-Publication Data

Guidelines on the instruments of the orchestra / by Lee Ching Ching
ISBN 967-985-481-7
1. Musical instruments – Handbooks, manuals, etc.
2. Instrumentation and orchestration – Handbooks, manuals, etc.
I. Title
784.19

Order No.: MPG-4010

Dedicated to my mother

Au Wai Hing

for her continual love, unwavering support,
wisdom and most of all,
for being there,
every step of the way.

CONTENTS

ACKNOWLEDGEMENT

My deepest appreciation to:

Mr. Loo Bang Hean
- *for his incisive review of the manuscript*

Mrs F. H. Monerasinghe
- *for her competent checking of grammatical errors in the language*

I would also like to acknowledge a list of friends and former teachers who had read this work at its various stages of completion, for their invaluable comments and suggestions. However, I would be solely responsible for any errors in this completed work.

Finally, an unstinting wealth of gratitude and love to my father Lee Kok Chye, my mother, my sister Wern Wern and my brother Lee Cheh for their unflagging support. In them, I have been blessed with two of life's most precious gifts - selfless love and eternal friendship.

"All good things come from God most high"

Lee Ching Ching
李青青
1996

PREFACE

This book is written to provide the necessary information to meet the syllabus requirement of music examinations. It can be used by both the music students as well as the amateur reader who are keen on knowing more about the instruments of the orchestra.

Each chapter has been arranged in a systematic and simple manner to assist students overcome any difficulties in searching for information in their revision.

Where relevant, noteworthy musical information have been grouped in a table to further assist the examination candidates in remembering the main facts.

It should, however, be noted that the reader's study of the musical instruments would be incomplete unless he is able to hear and relate to the timbre and tonal quality of each individual instrument. As such, this book should be used in conjunction with listening to the musical instruments either on tape or by attending musical concerts.

1. SOUND PRODUCTION

1. **Vibration causes sound.**

   Regular vibration produces musical notes while irregular vibration produces noise.

2. The pitch of a note is determined by the number of vibrations per second.

   - The pitch of a note produced by the stringed instruments depend on
     i.   the length of the string   -   the shorter the string, the higher the pitch.
     ii. the tension in the string   -   the tighter the string, the higher the pitch.
     iii. the thickness of the string   -   the thicker the string, the lower the pitch.

   - The pitch of a note produced by the wind instruments depend on the length of the vibrating air-column - the longer the length, the lower the pitch.

Note of interest:	The *highest* pitched instrument in the		
	• String family	-	violin
	• Woodwind family	-	piccolo
	• Brass family	-	trumpet
	The *lowest* pitched instrument in the		
	• String family	-	double bass
	• Woodwind family	-	double bassoon
	• Brass family	-	tuba

2. THE STRING FAMILY

The string section of the orchestra is made up of
a. Violin   b. Viola   c. Cello   d. Double bass

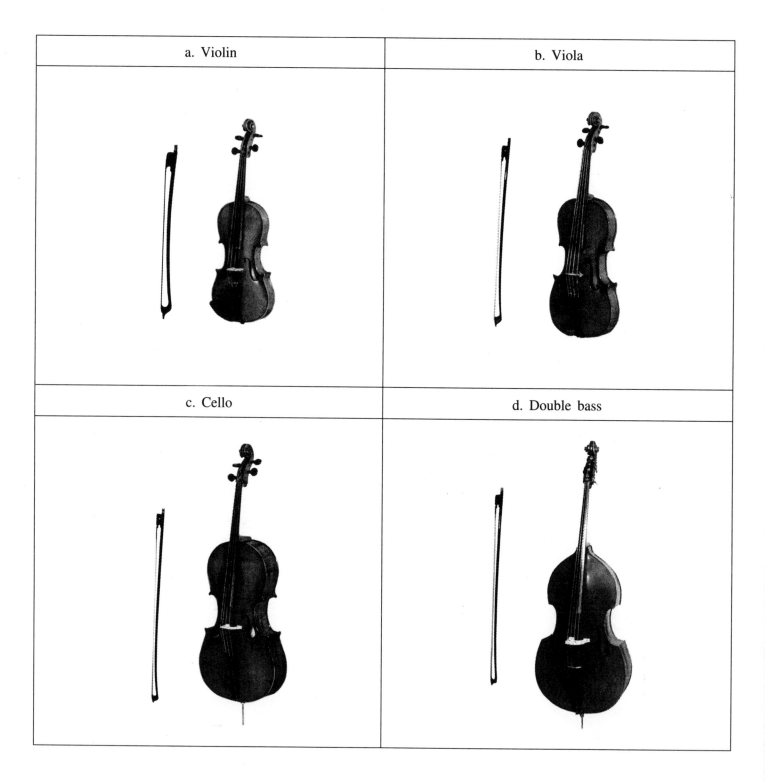

The Instruments

VIOLIN

1. The violin is the smallest in size and highest sounding instrument in the string family.

2. Supported between the chin and the left shoulder, the violin is played with a bow.

3. It has four strings.
   The *open strings are tuned a perfect fifth apart to G, D, A and E.

4. The treble clef is used in writing for the violin part.

5. The violin is a non-transposing instrument.

6. The violin makes up the largest number of players in the orchestra.
   They are divided into the first and second violins, both playing different musical parts.

7. The first violin usually carries the main thematic role while the second violin usually accompanies.
   In the classical period, it is very common for the second violin to double the first violin in unison or octaves.

8. The violin is capable of producing a wide range of tones which have an expressive and sparkling quality.

9. Foreign name for the violin:
   a. Geige or Violine - German
   b. Violon - French
   c. Violino - Italian

(*Open string: A string which is not stopped by the finger. This is the string that the instrument is tuned to.)

VIOLA

1. The viola is slightly larger than the violin and is also held in the same way as the violin. It uses a thicker bow.

2. It has four strings.
    The open strings are tuned a perfect fifth apart to C, G, D and A.

3. The alto clef is usually used in writing for the viola part.
    Sometimes, the treble clef is used for writing notes in the higher range to avoid the use of too many leger lines.

4. The viola is a non-transposing instrument.

5. The viola is capable of producing a mellow and deeply warm tone.

6. Due to its pitch and tone quality, the viola is easily drowned by accompanying parts, therefore, it is not often used as a solo instrument.
    However, it was given more melodious parts to play (sometimes even solo parts) since the time of Berlioz.

7. Foreign names for the viola:
    a. Bratsche - German
    b. Alto - French
    c. Viola - Italian

VIOLONCELLO

1. The violoncello is more commonly known by its short name, the cello.

2. Placed between the knees, it is supported by an adjustable peg which stands on the floor.

3. It has four strings.
   The open strings are tuned a perfect fifth apart to C, G, D and A.

4. The bass clef is commonly used in writing for the cello part.
   For notes in the higher range, the tenor clef and sometimes, even the treble clef is used.

5. The cello is a non-transposing instrument.

6. It is capable of producing an expressive and sonorous singing tone.
   As such, the cello is used to play solo melodic parts.

7. The cello is also commonly used to play the bass parts, either alone or with the double bass (in unison or octaves).

8. Foreign names for the cello:
   a. Violoncello - German
   b. Violoncelle - French
   c. Violoncello - Italian

DOUBLE BASS

1. The double bass is the largest in size and lowest sounding instrument in the string family.

2. The player has to stand or perch on a stool to support the double bass with his body and left knee.

3. It has four strings.
    The open strings are tuned a perfect fourth apart to E, A, D and G.

4. The lower range of the double bass can be extended by the following methods:
    a. Adding a fifth string which is tuned to the 'B' or 'C' note below the lowest open 'E' string.
    b. Fitting a device to the lowest open 'E' string to lower its pitch.
    c. By re-tuning the lowest open 'E' string to a lower pitch.
        This is known as 'scordatura'.

5. The bass clef is commonly used in writing for the double bass part.
    The tenor and the treble clef (though very rarely) is sometimes used for writing notes in the higher range.

6. The double bass is a transposing instrument with notes sounding an octave lower than the written ones.

7. The main duty of the double bass is to provide the bass line to the orchestra by playing the same notes as the cello part.
    (The bass part produced will sound an octave lower than the cello part as the double bass is a transposing instrument sounding an octave lower than the written notes.)

8. The 'pizzicato' is very effective when played on the double bass. However, the double bass is not very effective for playing 'double stopping' or 'finger-tremolo'.

9. Foreign name for the double bass:
    a. Kontrabass   - German
    b. Contrebasse - French
    c. Contrabasso - Italian

General Information

1. The most commonly used string combinations are:
    a. String quartet
    b. String orchestra

2. The sound on a string instrument is produced when the string is made to vibrate either by
    a. drawing a horse-hair bow across the string
    b. plucking the strings with the fingers, or
    c. tapping the strings with the wooden part of the bow.

3. An open string is a string which is not stopped by the finger.
    This is the string that the instrument is tuned to.

4. A stopped string is a string which is shortened by placing the fingers on the fingerboard
    to obtain different melodic notes.

5. Note that the larger the instrument, the shorter and thicker the bow used will be.

6. The pitch of the stringed instruments can be related in the following order:
    a. Violin   -   high
    b. Viola   -   moderate
    c. Cello   -   deep
    d. Double Bass   -   very deep

Various Methods of Playing the Stringed Instruments

Bow Mark

1. The direction of the bow's movement can be indicated on the score:
   a. Up-bow   : A movement of the bow from the point to heel.

   Indicated by the sign "V".

   b. Down-bow : A movement of the bow from the heel to the point.

   Indicated by the sign "⊓".

   c. A slur in string music only indicates the bowing, *not* the phrasing.
      i. If slurs are indicated, the notes within one slur are to be played in one single stroke of the bow, either up or down.
      ii. If unslurred, each note will be separately bowed, alternating between up-bow and down-bow.

   - As indicated by "V", the first note is played with an up-bow.
   - The next three notes are within one slur, so they are played in one downward bow.
   - The 'D' dotted crotchet note is played with an up-bow.
   - The next three 'E-F-E' quavers are played with a down-bow.
   - The following three 'D-E-D' quavers are unslurred,

     so the 'D' note is played with an up-bow,

     the 'E' note a down-bow and the 'D' note an up-bow.
   - The last note is played with a down-bow.

Multiple Stops

a. ***Double Stopping**   -   Stopping and bowing on two strings at a time.

(The 'E' note on the 'D' string and the 'C' note on the 'A' string are played at the same time.)

b. ***Triple Stopping**   -   Three strings are played from the lowest one upwards in a quick arpeggio to form a three-note chord.
(The bow can only be drawn across two strings at any one time.)

(Either the top two notes or the top note is held.)

c. ***Quadruple Stopping**   -   Four strings are played from the lowest one upwards in a quick arpeggio to form a four-note chord.

(*These terms are used even when one or more of the notes is an open string.)

Harmonics

1. This is a musical effect obtained by lightly touching a vibrating string at certain points (*nodes) along its length instead of firmly pressing the string down on the fingerboard.
   Node is the resting point between two vibrating parts.

2. There are two kinds of harmonics:
   a. Natural harmonics : this is produced by touching the node of an open string.
   b. Artificial harmonics : this is produced by touching the node of a stopped string.

3. Below are examples of notations used to indicate harmonics.

   ** (i)    (ii)    (iii)

   - Examples (i) and (ii) will produce notes sounding two octaves higher:

   - Example (iii) - The string is *stopped* to obtain the note 'G' and is *touched* at the note indicated (diamond-shaped) to produce a note sounding two octaves higher than the stopped note, 'G':

   ** *Note that the symbol ° is also used to indicate the open string of an instrument.*
   When used to indicate harmonics, the ° can be placed over notes other than the notes of the open string or it can appear over a series of notes:

   (However, an oval "o" is used nowadays for open string and "°" for harmonics.)

4. Foreign terms indicating harmonics are:
   a. Flageolettone   - German
   b. Sons harmoniques - French
   c. Armonici   - Italian

Tremolo

1. This is a musical effect obtained by

    a.   playing a single note with rapid alternating bow strokes.
        This is known as bow-tremolo, or

    b. *rapidly alternating between two different notes on the same string.
        This is known as finger-tremolo.

> *For a finger-tremolo, the interval between the two notes should not be larger than*
>   *i. a fourth for the violin and viola*
>   *ii. a third for the cello*

2. Tremolo is indicated by strokes drawn across the stem of a note.
   The number of strokes present depends on the time value of the note.
   Below are examples of notation used to indicate

    a. bow-tremolo (tremolo on a single note) :

        OR   OR

    b. finger-tremolo (tremolo between two different notes) :

        OR   OR

Mutes

1. This is a device which is fixed onto the bridge of a string instrument to absorb some vibrations, thus enabling the strings to play softly.

2. Muting is also used to create special tone colour.
    Sometimes, a passage marked 'forte' is deliberately played with the mute on to produce a desired musical effect.

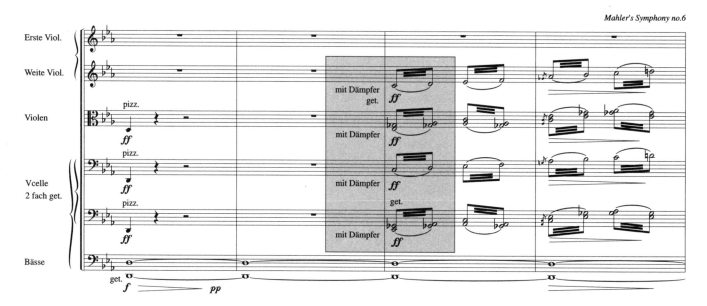

The mute is deliberately used to play 'ff' to create a special tone colour.

3. Foreign terms to indicate '***use the mute***':

    a. mit Dampfer or Gedampft - German
    b. avec sourdines - French
    c. con sordina or con sordino - Italian

    (Plural : sordine or sordini)

4. Foreign terms to indicate '***remove the mute***':

    a. ohne Dampfer or Dampfer weg - German
    b. sans sourdines or otez les sourdines - French
    c. senze sordini or via sordini - Italian

Performance Direction

1. Arco — Resume the use of the bow after a passage of pizzicato.

2. A2 or zu2 — Players are to divide into two groups, each playing one part.
    E.g.: 'a3' means players are to divide into three groups.

3. Col Legno — The wood of the bow is used.

4. Con Sordini (con sord.) — With the mute.

5. Double Stopping — Stopping and playing on two strings at a time.

6. *Detache — Play each note in a non-legato manner.

7. Divisi (div.) — To divide into two or more groups.
    E.g.: 'Divisi a3' means divide into three groups.

8. Flautato (flautando) — Apply natural harmonics to the note.

9. Glissando (gliss.) — Rapid sliding of the finger along the string.

10. Harmonics — This is a musical effect obtained by lightly touching a vibrating
    string at certain points along its length.

11. *Loure — Play each note slightly detached with a light accent.

12. *Martellato (Martele) — Hammered. Playing each note separately and firmly.

13. Naturale — Resume bowing in the ordinary position.
    (Usually used after the term 'Sul Ponticello')

14. Non-divisi — Do not divide into groups.

15. Portamento — Playing two different notes on the same string by gliding the
    finger along the two positions.

16. Quadruple Stopping — Playing four strings from the lowest one upwards in a quick
    arpeggio to form a four-note chord.

17. *Saltando (saltato) — Bouncing the bow up and down on the string to produce a light effect.

18. *Sautille	-	A lighter form of 'spiccato'.
19. Scordatura	-	An instruction to retune the strings to different notes.
20. Senza Sordini (senza sord.)	-	Without the mute.
21. *Spiccato	-	Making each note light and short.
22. Sul G	-	On the G string Sul D : On the D string. Sul A : On the A string. Sul E : On the E string.
23. Sul Ponticello	-	Bowing the strings very near or on the bridge.
24. Sul Tasto (Sur la touche)	-	Bowing the strings very near the fingerboard.
25. Tremolo (trem.)	-	Quivering the bow very rapidly to produce a shivering effect.
26. Triple Stopping	-	Playing three strings from the lowest one upwards in a quick arpeggio to form a three-note chord.
27. Unisono (unis.)	-	All performers play the same note after a 'divisi' passage.
28. Vibrato	-	Stopping the string by shaking the left hand to make the tone warmer.
29. V	-	Up-bow.
30. ⊓	-	Down-bow.
31.	-	This curved line means that the notes within are to be played in one single bow stroke.

There is no particular need to know in depth the various bow strokes indicated by these terms because notes can be played in many varying forms of legato and staccato. Also, edited markings need not be literally followed in the performance as this is subjective to the musical experience and interpretation of the player.

Term	Symbol
Tremolo	𝅘𝅥 or 𝅘𝅥
Harmonics	◇ or °
Open String	(treble clef with note marked 0)
Portamento	(notes connected by straight line)
Glissando	(notes connected by straight line)

Note of interest:

1. The difference between the symbol ° for harmonics and open string is that harmonics is indicated by the presence of a continuous row of ° while open string is indicated by the presence of the symbol ° at odd notes.
   (Nowadays, an oval " **o** " is used to indicate open string.)

   Example:

   HARMONICS   OPEN STRING

2. The difference between the symbol used for portamento and glissando is that ***portamento*** is used to link the ***melodic tones*** together while ***glissando*** covers a fairly **wide interval** between two notes. (see table above)

3. In an orchestral **string** score, note the direction of the stems used.

   a.   b.

   a. The notes are played by double stopping.

   b. The notes are played by two groups of players with each group playing different notes, i.e., a group playing notes with the stems upwards and another playing notes with the stems downwards.

Score Reading

1. The stringed instruments are placed at the bottom of the full orchestral score in this arrangement:

   Violin

   Viola

   Violoncello

   Double bass

2. If the string part is written with notes having stems pointing in different directions, the players are to divide into groups, each playing a different note.

   Example:

   This indicates that the 'D' note is played by one group of players and the 'F' note by another group.

3. If a part is to be played in unison, the part will be written as

   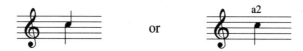

   or

4. To indicate double stopping, the term 'non-divisi' (or 'Doppelgriff' in German) is used.

   Another way of indicating this is to have the parts written as   with both the notes having stems in the same direction.

Summary For Revision

Instrument	Clef	Transposing	Open String
Violin	Treble Treble (for high notes	No	G — 4th string, D — 3rd string, A — 2nd string, E — 1st string
Viola	Alto Treble (for high notes)	No	C — 4th string, G — 3rd string, D — 2nd string, A — 1st string
Violoncello	Bass Tenor Treble (for high notes)	No	C — 4th string, G — 3rd string, D — 2nd string, A — 1st string
Double Bass	Bass Tenor Treble (very rare)	Yes, it sounds an octave lower than written.	E — 4th string, A — 3rd string, D — 2nd string, G — 1st string (8ve)

The G - string can be indicated as Sul G or Sul IV.
The D - string can be indicated as Sul D or Sul III.
This is likewise for the other strings.

*Range of notes for each string instrument.

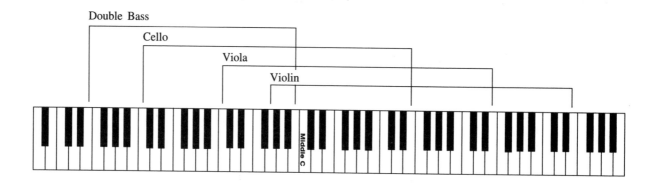

1. The thickest open string is the lowest of the given range for each stringed instrument.

2. The **highest note** of the range given above is only an estimation because a more skilful player can reach a higher note.

*The range of an instrument is the limits between the lower and upper register.

Foreign Terms For The Orhestral Instruments

FAMILY	ENGLISH	FRENCH	ITALIAN	GERMAN
String	Violin (vln.)	Violon (vln., vns., vons.)	Violino (v., vl., vln., vni.)	Violine or Geige (V., Vl., Vln.)
	Viola (vla.)	Alto (a.)	Viola (va., vla., vle.)	Bratsche (Br.)
	Cello (vc., vcl.)	Violoncelle (vc., velles.)	Violoncello (vc., vcl., vlc.)	Violoncell (Vc., Vlc.)
	Double Bass (d.b., d.bs.)	Contrebasse (cb., c.b.)	Contrabasso or Basso (cb., c.b., b.)	Kontrabass (Kb.)

3. THE WOODWIND FAMILY

The woodwind section of the orchestra is made up of

*Flute	Piccolo
*Oboe	Cor Anglais
*Clarinet	Bass Clarinet
*Bassoon	Double Bassoon
	Saxophone
	Alto Flute

*These are the four main woodwind instruments.

Flute	Oboe	Clarinet	Bassoon	Piccolo
Cor Anglais	Bass Clarinet	Double Bassoon	Saxophone	Alto Flute

The Instruments

FLUTE

1. It has no reed and its part is written in the treble clef.

2. The flute is held sideways and the player blows through a mouth hole in the side.

3. The notes in the lower range is warm and velvety while the notes in the upper range are brilliant.

4. A technique known as 'overblowing' will produce notes at an octave higher.

5. The flute is very agile and is often used to play rapid scalic and arpeggio passages.

6. The flute is a non-transposing instrument.

7. Foreign name for the flute:
   a. Flote or Grosse Flote   -   German
   b. Flute or Grande Flute   -   French
   c. Flauto or Flauto Grande -   Italian

ALTO FLUTE

1. It has no reed and its part is written in the treble clef.

2. The alto flute is only occasionally used in the orchestra.

3. Pitched in 'G', the alto flute is also known as the 'bass flute' or the 'flute in G'.

4. It is a transposing instrument with notes sounding a perfect fourth lower than written.

5. The notes in the lower range is very warm and rich in tone while its upper notes lack in brilliance.

6. Foreign name for the alto flute:

    a. Altflote   - German
    b. Flute en Sol.   - French
    c. Flauto Contralto - Italian

PICCOLO

1. It has no reed and its part is written in the treble clef.

2. The piccolo is the highest sounding instrument in the orchestra.
    Its old name is 'octave flute'.

3. It is a transposing instrument with notes sounding an octave higher than written.

4. The piccolo is not consistently used throughout an orchestral piece, as such,
    its part is often played by the *second* or *third* flautist.

5. It is commonly used for special musical effects or for adding brilliance to an orchestral tutti.

6. The upper notes of the piccolo are bright and piercing in tone.

7. Foreign name for the piccolo:

    a. Kleine Flote   - German
    b. Petite Flute   - French
    c. Flauto Piccolo or Ottavino - Italian

OBOE

1. It uses a double reed and its part is written in the treble clef.

2. The oboe is *non-transposing.

   It plays the standard 'A' note for the orchestra to tune to.

   However, note that the oboe in E flat sounds a minor third higher than written.

3. The oboe d'amore is another type of oboe much favoured by Bach but is only occasionally used in the orchestra now.

   It is a transposing instrument pitched in 'A' and sounds a minor 3rd lower than written.

4. Foreign name for the oboe:
   a. Oboe or Hoboe - German
   b. Hautbois - French
   c. Oboe - Italian

COR ANGLAIS

1. It uses a double reed and its part is written in the treble clef.

2. The cor anglais is also known as the English horn.

3. It is a transposing instrument pitched in 'F' and sounds a perfect 5th lower than written.

4. The cor anglais is occasionally given a solo melodic part in the orchestra.

   Its part is often played by the *second* oboist (who will resume playing the oboe after the solo cor anglais part.)

5. It is capable of producing a warm and deep, reedy tone.

6. Foreign name for the cor anglais:
   a. English Horn - German
   b. Cor anglais - French
   c. Corno Inglese - Italian

CLARINET

1. The clarinet is a single reed instrument and its part is written in the treble clef.

2. Clarionet is the old spelling of clarinet.

3. The following is a table on the list of members of the clarinet family and their interval of transposition.

Instrument	Interval of transposition
1. Clarinet in C	1. Non-transposing
2. Clarinet in D	2. Sounds a major 2nd higher
3. *Clarinet in E flat	3. Sounds a minor 3rd higher
4. *Clarinet in A	4. Sounds a minor 3rd lower
5. *Clarinet in B flat	5. Sounds a major 2nd lower
6. Basset horn (pitched in F)	6. Sounds a perfect 5th lower
7. *Bass clarinet in B flat	7. Sounds a major 9th lower
8. Bass clarinet in A	8. Sounds a minor 10th lower

These are the more regularly used members of the clarinet family though the clarinet in A and in B flat are more commonly used in the symphony orchestra.

- The clarinet in C was widely used in the music of the 18th and 19th century but is now being replaced by either the clarinet in A or B flat.
- The clarinet in B flat is more suitable for music in the flat keys.
- The clarinet in A is more suitable for music in the sharp keys.
- The clarinet in D is very rarely used.
- The clarinet in E flat is the smallest member of the clarinet family.
  It was usually found in the military bands but was occasionally used in the symphony orchestra since the time of Berlioz.
- The parts for both the bass clarinets in A and B flat are written in the treble clef.
- Basset horn, though rarely used now, was much favoured by Mozart.
  Foreign name for the basset horn: i.   **Basset horn**   -   **German**
  ii.   **Cor de basset**   -   **French**
  iii.   **Corno di bassetto**   -   **Italian**
  or Corno bassetto

4. Though the clarinet was invented in the early 18th century, it was only at around 1770 that Mozart established its use in the orchestra.

5. The chalumeau refers to the lower register of the clarinet and the tone colour of this part is deep and rich.

6. The tone of the middle register is sweet and mellow but as the pitch goes higher, the tone becomes rather squealing.

7. Foreign name for the clarinet: a. Klarinette - German
                                    b. Clarinette - French
                                    c. Clarinetto - Italian

BASSOON

1. It uses a double reed and its part is commonly written in the bass clef.
   The tenor and the treble clef (though very rarely) are used for writing higher notes.

2. It is a non-transposing instrument.

3. The tone of the lowest register is deep and sonorous, the middle register is expressive and subdued while the higher register tends to be tight and shrill.

4. Foreign name for the bassoon: a. Fagott   - German
                                   b. Basson   - French
                                   c. Fagotto - Italian

DOUBLE BASSOON

1. It uses a double reed and its part is written in the bass clef.

2. The double bassoon is also known as the contrabassoon and is the lowest pitched instrument in the woodwind family.

3. It is a transposing instrument with notes sounding an octave lower than written.

4. It is used to play the bass-line of the orchestra by either doubling the bassoon part at an octave lower or reinforcing the double bass part.

5. It is capable of producing a deep and sonorous tone.

6. Sometimes, the double bassoon part is played by the *second* bassoon player.

7. Foreign name for the double bassoon: a. Kontrafagott - German
                                                    b. Contrebasson - French
                                                    c. Contrafagotto - Italian

SAXOPHONE

1. It uses a single reed and its part is written in the treble clef.

2. The saxophone was invented round about 1840 by Adolphe Sax.

3. It is rarely used in the orchestra and is more popularly used in jazz bands.

4. The following is a table on the list of members of the saxophone family and their interval of transposition.

Instrument	Interval of transposition
1. *Soprano saxophone in B flat	1. Sounds a major 2nd lower
2. *Alto saxophone in E flat	2. Sounds a major 6th lower
3. *Tenor saxophone in B flat	3. Sounds a major 9th lower
4. *Baritone saxophone in E flat	4. Sounds a major 13th lower

These four instruments form the saxophone quartet.

5. The alto saxophone is the most commonly used, followed by the tenor saxophone.

6. The saxophone part is always written in the treble clef, even for the alto, tenor and baritone saxophones.

7. It has a smooth, sentimental and singing tone quality.

8. Foreign name for the saxophone: a. Saxophon   - German
                                            b. Saxophone   - French
                                            c. Saxofono or Sassofono - Italian

General Information

1. The sound on a woodwind instrument is produced when the air in the hollow column of the tube
    is made to vibrate by
    a. blowing a stream of air through the mouthpiece, or
    b. making a single or double reed vibrate.

2. A reed is a very thin slice of cane which is fixed over the mouthpiece.
    It produces sound when it is made to vibrate by a player's breath.

3. There are two kinds of reed:
    a. Single reed   : This is a single piece of cane which vibrates against the mouthpiece.
    b. Double reed   : These are two pieces of cane which vibrate against one another.

4. The pitch of the note produced depends on the length of the vibrating air column;
    the longer the column, the lower the pitch.

5. The woodwind instruments can be divided into three categories:

No Reed	Single Reed	Double Reed
1. Flute 2. Piccolo	1. Clarinet 2. Bass clarinet 3. Saxophone	1. Oboe 2. Cor Anglais 3. Bassoon 4. Double bassoon

6. In a very large orchestra, the players of the main woodwind instruments are sometimes required to play
    an extra instrument. These extra instruments are known as the auxiliary (additional) instruments.

The main woodwind instruments also play:	
Main Woodwind	*Auxiliary Woodwind:*
1. Flute ⟶	Piccolo (small flute)
2. Oboe ⟶	Cor Anglais (larger oboe)
3. Clarinet ⟶	Bass clarinet (larger clarinet)
4. Bassoon ⟶	Double bassoon (larger bassoon)

Various Methods of Playing the Woodwind Instruments

1. Tonguing   -   A method of tone production whereby the player controls the flow of air by silently speaking the syllable 'tu' or 'du'.

2. Double Tonguing   -   A technique used to play *fast staccato* passages by silently speaking 'tu-ku-tu-ku' while blowing into the mouthpiece.

3. Triple Tonguing   -   A technique used to play *fast staccato triplet* passages by silently speaking 'tu-ku-tu' or 'tu-tu-ku' while blowing into the mouthpiece.

4. Flatterzunge (Flzg.)   -   A technique used to play *fast chromatic* passages by rolling an 'r' with the tongue while blowing into the mouthpiece.

   Symbol:

5. Two or more notes within a slur are to be played in one breath of air.
   Notes which are not slurred are tongued separately.

6. Overblowing   -   A technique used to produce notes at an octave higher by adjusting the lip pressure and breath while repeating the same fingering used for notes in the lower octave.
   All the woodwind instruments overblow at an octave, except for the clarinet which overblows at a perfect 12th.

7. Mutes   -   *No mutes* are used by the woodwind instruments.

Score Reading

1. The woodwind instruments are placed at the top of the full orchestral score in this arrangement:

   Piccolo

   Flute

   Oboe

   Cor Anglais

   Clarinet

   Bass clarinet

   Bassoon

   Double bassoon

2. When two of a same instrument are used (e.g.: 2 flutes), the *first and second parts are written on one stave. The stem of the first part points upwards while the stem of the second part points downwards.

   Only in cases where the rhythm is complicated will each of these parts use an individual stave.

3. When only the first part is playing, the second part will be represented by a rest.
   Alternatively, the symbol '1' or 'I' may be used to mark the first part.

　　　　**OR**　　　　

4. Similarly, when only the second part is playing, there will be a rest in the first part.
   Alternatively, the symbol '2' or 'II' may be used to mark the second part.

　　　　**OR**　　　　

5. The term 'divisi' and 'unis' are **NOT** used by the woodwind instruments.

6. The melodic or thematic material is generally given to the flute, oboe, clarinet, piccolo and cor anglais while the bass clarinet, bassoon and double bassoon are generally used to support the harmony.

Summary For Revision

Instrument	Reed	*Transposing	Clef
Flute	No reed	No	Treble
Alto Flute	No reed	Yes	Treble
Piccolo	No reed	Yes	Treble
Oboe	Double	No	Treble
Cor Anglais	Double	Yes	Treble
Clarinet	Single	Yes	Treble
Bass clarinet	Single	Yes	Treble Bass (at times)
Bassoon	Double	No	Bass Tenor Treble (very rare)
Double bassoon	Double	Yes	Bass
Saxophone	Single	Yes	Treble

For the woodwind instruments which transpose, please refer to the individual section for the interval of transposition.

Range of notes for each woodwind instrument.

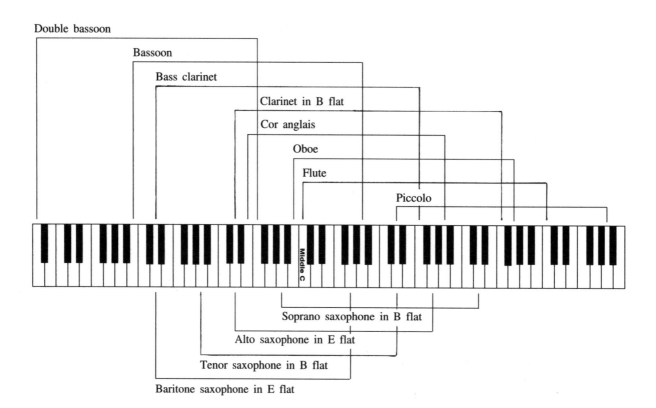

The *highest note* of the range given above is only an estimation because a more skilful player can reach a higher note.

Foreign Terms For The Orchestral Instruments

FAMILY	ENGLISH	FRENCH	ITALIAN	GERMAN
Woodwind	Piccolo (picc.)	Petite flute (pte.fl.)	Flauto piccolo (fl.picc. or ottavino)	Kleine flöte (kl.fl.)
	Flute (fl.)	Flute (fl.) or Grande flute (gde.fl.)	Flauto (fl.) or Flauto grande (fl.gr.)	Flöte (fl.) or Grosse flöte (Gr.fl.)
	Oboe (ob.)	Hautbois (hb., htb.)	Oboe (ob.)	Hoboe (hb.)
	English horn (E.H.) or Cor anglais (C.A.)	Cor anglais (C.A.)	Corno inglese (C.I. or cor.ingl.)	Englisches horn (E.H., Engl.Hr.)
	Clarinet (c., cl., clt.)	Clarinette (cl.)	Clarinetto (cl., clar.)	Klarinette (kl., klar.)
	Bass clarinet (b.cl.)	Clarinette basse (cl.b.)	Clarinetto basso (cl.b. or clarone)	Bassklarinette (bkl.)
	Bassoon (bsn.)	Bassoon (bn., bon., bssn.)	Fagotto (fg., fag.)	Fagott (fg., fag.)
	Double Bassoon or Contrabassoon (d.bsn., c.bsn.)	Contrebasson (cbn., c.bon.)	Contrafagotto (Cfg., c.fag.)	Kontrafagott (k.fag.)

4. THE BRASS FAMILY

The brass section is made up of

*Horn   Cornet

*Trumpet

*Trombone

*Tuba

*These are the four main brass instruments.

Horn	Tuba	Cornet

Trumpet	Trombone

The Instruments

HORN

1. It uses valves and its part is mostly written in the treble clef.
    The bass clef is used where convenient.

2. All horns transpose *downwards*, with parts sounding lower than written.

3. The standard orchestra commonly uses *four horns.
    They appear in pairs with
    a. the first and the third horns playing the higher melodic part, and
    b. the second and the fourth horns playing the lower melodic part.
    A larger orchestra may use up to eight horns.

4. The following is a table on the interval of transposition for the members of the
    horn family which are pitched in different keys.

Instrument	Interval of transposition
1. Horn in C	1. Sounds an octave lower
2. Horn in D	2. Sounds a minor 7th lower
3. Horn in E flat	3. Sounds a major 6th lower
4. Horn in E	4. Sounds a minor 6th lower
5. **Horn in F (French horn)	5. Sounds a perfect 5th lower
6. Horn in G	6. Sounds a perfect 4th lower
7. Horn in A flat	7. Sounds a major 3rd lower
8. Horn in A	8. Sounds a minor 3rd lower
9. Horn in B flat	9. Sounds a major 9th lower
10. Alto horn in B flat	10. Sounds a major 2nd lower

**This is the most commonly used horn.*

5. Foreign name for the horn:
    a. Horn - German
    b. Cor - French
    c. Corno - Italian

TRUMPET

1. It uses valves and its part is written in the treble clef.

2. The trumpet is the highest sounding instrument in the brass section.

3. a. Before the valve was invented, the natural trumpet (without valves) could only play certain notes and keys.
   b. With the invention of the valve in the early 19th century, the trumpet is able to play all the notes of the scale.

4. In the Baroque period, the trumpet parts often covered very high notes.
   To obtain notes from the higher range, a technique known as **clarino playing** was devoloped, using varying lip tension and breath control.

5. The trumpet is capable of producing a bright, full and powerful tone.

6. It is most effectively used in
   a. tutti passages
   b. fanfare passages
   c. emphasizing dotted rhythmic features such as ♪. ♪ , etc.

7. It is a transposing instrument. The following is a table on the interval of transposition for the members of the trumpet family which are pitched in different keys.

Instrument	Interval of transposition
1. *Trumpet in C	1. Non-transposing
2. Trumpet in D	2. Sounds a major 2nd higher
3. Trumpet in E flat	3. Sounds a minor 3rd higher
4. Trumpet in E	4. Sounds a major 3rd higher
5. Trumpet in F	5. Sounds a perfect 4th higher
6. Trumpet in B	6. Sounds a minor 2nd lower
7. *Trumpet in B flat	7. Sounds a major 2nd lower
8. *Trumpet in A	8. Sounds a minor 3rd lower

*These are the more commonly used trumpets.

8. Foreign name for the trumpet:
   a. Trompete - German
   b. Trompette - French
   c. Tromba - Italian

CORNET

1. It uses valves and its part is written in the treble clef.

2. It was invented in **France** around **1825** and is only occasionally used in the orchestra
   * *The use of cornet in a work implies*
     a. *a French composer.*
     b. *the estimated date of composition.*

3. The tone produced by the cornet is a blend of both the tone of the trumpet and the horn.

4. It is a transposing instrument.
   a. Cornet in B flat sounds a major 2nd lower.
   b. Cornet in E flat sounds a minor 3rd lower.

5. Foreign name for the cornet:
   a. Kornett   - German
   b. Cornet a pistons or Piston - French
   c. Cornetta   - Italian

TROMBONE

1. It uses a slide and its part is written in the bass clef.
   For the higher notes, the tenor clef is sometimes used.

2. By using the slide which has seven different positions, the trombone is able to play all the notes of the chromatic scale.

3. The musical effect 'glissando' can be easily played on the trombone.

4. It is a non-transposing instrument.

5. a. The standard orchestra commonly uses *two tenor* and *one bass* trombone.
   b. The trombones are very commonly used together with the tuba to form a four-part harmony. When used, *the tuba usually shares a stave with the bass trombone.*

6. The earliest form of trombone existed round about the 15th century but it was Beethoven who first established the use of the trombone in the symphony orchestra.

7. Foreign name for the trombone:
   a. Posaune   - German
   b. Trombone - French and Italian

TUBA

1. It uses valves and its part is written in the bass clef.

2. The tuba is the lowest sounding instruments in the brass section.

3. It is a non-transposing instrument

4. The tuba was developed round about 1850.

5. The tuba family is a very large one. The tuba which is usually used in the standard orchestra is the **bass tuba in F**.

6. The bass tuba was used only from around 1875 to replace the *ophicleide.
   The ophicleide was commonly used in the mid-19th century but is no longer in use now.

7. Its main duty is to play the bass line by doubling either the **fourth horn** or the **bass trombone** at an octave lower.

8. Foreign name for the tuba: Tuba - German, French and Italian.

General Information

1. The sound on a brass instrument is produced when the column of air blown into the mouthpiece is made to vibrate in the tube.

2. Different notes on the brass instruments can be obtained by varying the length of the tube.
   a. In olden times, a crook is used to add extra length of tubing.
   b. With the invention of valves in the early 19th century, the crooks were gradually replaced.

3. By changing the lip pressure, a set of notes called the harmonic series can be produced by the brass player.

4. By using a slide or valves, all the others notes between the harmonic series can be produced.

5. The pitch of the note produced depends on the length of the tube; the longer the tube, the lower the pitch.

6. Depending on the shape of the tube, the brass instruments can be divided into two categories:
   a. cylindrical tube - trumpet, trombone.
   b. conical tube   - horn, tuba
   The tube of the cornet is partly cylindrical and partly conical.

Various Methods of Playing the Brass Instruments

1. Mutes
   - a. The brass instruments are muted by inserting a pear-shaped mute into the bell.
   - b. The horn players can also apply muting by pushing the right hand into the bell to produce 'stopped' notes.
   - c. The use of mute softens the sound produced as well as changes the quality of tone produced.

This table below shows the different terms that could be used to refer to 'stopped note'.

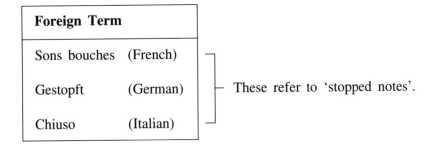

Foreign Term	
Sons bouches	(French)
Gestopft	(German)
Chiuso	(Italian)

These refer to 'stopped notes'.

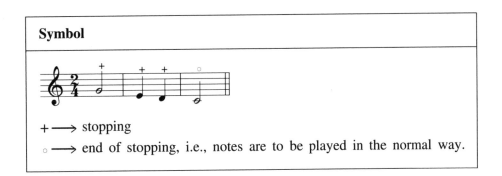

Symbol

+ ⟶ stopping

○ ⟶ end of stopping, i.e., notes are to be played in the normal way.

2. Cuivre
   - This is a technique used to produce a special musical effect by forcing the tone by blowing hard with the hand inside the bell of the horn.
   'Cuivre' can be used on open notes as well as stopped notes.

3. Glissando
   - This is a musical effect obtained by moving the slide while the trombone player blows into the mouthpiece.

4. Pavillon en l'air
   (Bell in the air)
   - This is a musical effect obtained by raising the bell of the instrument high in the air to produce a more prominent tone.

- Before the year 1850, the brass instruments use the *crook.*

- *Crook* is a device of metal tubings of different lengths that is added to the end of a mouthpiece so that a new set of notes, called the *harmonic series* can be obtained.

- Each crook produces a different harmonic series. Therefore, the player has to use several crooks in order to have a wider selection of notes to play.

- With the invention of valves in 1850, the brass instruments use the valve (piston) system.

- With this system, all notes from the chromatic scale can be obtained, thus, more melodic roles were given to the brass instruments.

Score Reading

1. The brass family is placed below the woodwind section of the full orchestral score in this arrangement:
   Horn
   Trumpet
   Trombone
   Tuba

2. No key-signature was used in the horn parts. It was only in the twentieth century that the use of key-signature in the horn parts was introduced.

3. When four horns were used, the first and third horns usually played the higher two of the four horn parts and not expected to play as low as the second and fourth horns.

4. When three trombones and one tuba were used, the first and second trombones share one stave (usually using the tenor clef) and the third trombone usually shares a stave with the tuba (usually using the bass clef).

5. From the Romantic onwards, many playing techniques such as using of mutes, the stopped effect for the horns, etc., were used for special musical effects.

Summary For Revision

Instrument	Sound Production	*Transposing	Clef	General
Horn	Valve	Yes	Tenor Bass	The horn pitched in 'F' is commonly used.
Trumpet	Valve	Yes	Treble	Highest sounding in the brass family.
Cornet	Valve	Yes	Treble	Only occasionally used.
Trombone	Slide	No	a. Tenor trombone: Bass clef and tenor clef. b. Bass Trombone: Bass clef	Standard number used in the orchestra: 2 tenor trombones 1 bass trombone
Tuba	Valve	No	Bass	Lowest sounding in the brass family.

*For the brass instruments which transpose, please refer to the individual section for the interval of transposition.

Range of notes for each brass instrument

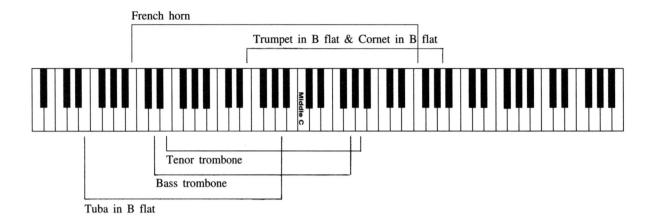

The *highest note* of the range given above is only an estimation because a more skilful player can reach a higher note.

Foreign Terms For The Orchestral Instruments

FAMILY	ENGLISH	FRENCH	ITALIAN	GERMAN
Brass	Horn (hn., hr.)	Cor	Corno (cor.)	Horn (hr., hrn.)
	Trumpet (tpt., trpt.)	Trompette (tromp., trp.)	Tromba (tr., tbe.)	Trompete (tr., trmp.)
	Cornet	Cornet à piston (corn.)	Cornetta	Kornett
	Trombone (tbn., trb., trom.)	Trombone (trb., trom.)	Trombone (tbn., trb., trbn., tbni.)	Posaune (pos., ps.)
	Tuba (tb., tba.)	Tuba (tb.)	Tuba (tb., tba.)	Tuba (tb.)

5. THE PERCUSSION FAMILY

1. The percussion instruments can be divided into two categories:

   a. Those with a definite pitch, on which a melody can be played.

   b. Those with an indefinite pitch, on which a melody cannot be played.

a.

Timpani	Xylophone	Tubular Bells	Glockenspiel

b.

Side drum	Cymbal	Maracas	Wooden block	Bongos

Definite Pitch/Tuned	Clef		Indefinite Pitch/Untuned
Timpani	Bass		Bass Drum
*Celesta	Treble and bass (in 2 staves)		Side Drum (Snare Drum)
*Xylophone	Treble		Cymbal
*Glockenspiel	Treble		Gong
*Vibraphone	Treble		Triangle
*Tubular Bells	Treble		*Tambourine
			*Castanets
			*Wooden Block
			*Maracas
			*Bongos
			*Sleigh Bells
			*Whip

*These are the percussion instruments which are seldom used in the orchestra.
 They are usually used for a special musical effect.

2. a. The percussion instruments with an indefinite pitch are usually used for rhythmic purposes and for tone colour.

   b. The parts for the indefinite pitch instruments are often written on single lines. However, a stave is sometimes used.

Britten's "The Young Person's
Guide To The Orchestra"

This is an example on how the percussion parts are notated in an orchestral score.

The Instruments

TIMPANI

1. The timpani are also commonly known as the kettledrums.
   Timpani is the plural of timpano. As it is always used in pairs, it is referred to as the timpani.

2. It is a tuned instrument and its part is written in the bass clef.
   The timpani can play notes of definite pitch but **not** a melody.

3. In the Baroque period, the timpani were often used together with the trumpet.

4. a. Initially, two timpani were used and they were tuned to the tonic and dominant of the scale.
    b. Now, three or four timpani are used and their pitch is often changed.

5. The timpani are commonly used to play single note, rhythmic group of notes and the thunderous rolls.

6. The glissando effect can also be produced by changing the pitch from one note to another by using the pedal while the drums are being played.

7. The timpani are very effective when used to add rhythmic intensity and colour to the music.

8. Sometimes, modern composers use a key-signature but in the olden days, the timpani parts were written without a key-signature - the tuning used would be stated at the beginning.

9. To indicate changes of tuning in the course of a movement, terms like 'muta G in A' (change tuning from G to A) is used.

10. To indicate a drum roll, the following indications are used.

11. Foreign name for the timpani:
    a. Pauken   - German
    b. Timbales - French
    c. Timpani   - Italian

CELESTA

1. The celesta is a tuned instrument and its part is written on two staves in the treble and bass clef (like the piano part).

2. It has a compass of four octaves with $\begin{array}{c}\text{𝄢 o}\end{array}$ as the lowest written note but sounding an octave higher.

3. It is rarely used in the orchestra.

XYLOPHONE

1. The xylophone is a tuned instrument and its part is written in the treble clef.

2. It has a set of wooden bars of different sizes which is arranged in two rows like a piano keyboard and is mounted in a case. It is played by striking the keys with a wooden mallet.

3. The notes produced sound an octave higher than written.

4. It is capable of producing a bright and dry tone quality.

5. Foreign name for the xylophone:
    a. Xylophon   - German
    b. Xylophone   - French
    c. Xilofono or Silofono - Italian

GLOCKENSPIEL

1. The glockenspiel is a tuned instrument and its part is written in the treble clef.

2. It is constructed similarly to the xylophone except that the bars are made of metal. It is played by striking the keys with a mallet with heads made of various material like rubber, wood or metal.

3. The notes produced sound two octaves higher than written.

4. It is capable of producing bell-like tone quality.

5. Foreign name for the glockenspiel:
    a. Glockenspiel   - German
    b. Jeu de timbres or Carillon - French
    c. Campanelli   - Italian

VIBRAPHONE

1. The vibraphone is a tuned instrument and its part is written in the treble clef.

2. It is constructed similarly to the glockenspiel except that it has a resonating tube beneath each metal bar.

3. The notes produced sound at its written pitch.

4. It is capable of producing a sweet, gentle and sustained tone quality.

TUBULAR BELLS

1. The bells is a tuned instrument and its part is written in the treble clef.

2. It is a series of steel tubes hanging from a wooden frame.
   It is played by striking the tubes with a wooden mallet.

3. Foreign name for the bells:
   a. Glocken   -   German
   b. Cloches   -   French
   c. Campane   -   Italian

BASS DRUM

1. It is an untuned instrument.

2. In the orchestra, the bass drum is supported in an upright position and is struck from the right hand side.

3. Foreign name for the bass drum:
   a. Grosse trommel   -   German
   b. Grosse caisse   -   French
   c. Cassa or Gran cassa -   Italian

SIDE DRUM

1. It is also known as the snare drum and it is an untuned instrument.

2. It is similarly shaped as the bass drum but is much smaller and is struck at the top, not from the side.

3. A device called 'snares' is stretched across beneath the surface of the drum and this enables
   a rattling effect to be obtained when the wooden sticks are used.

4. However, if the snares are not wanted, it can be indicated in the music as 'scordato' or 'senza corda'.

5. The 'roll' can be effectively played on the side drum.
   The roll is notated the same way as the timpani roll.

6. Foreign name for the side drum: a. Trommel   - German
                                     b. Caisse or Tambour - French
                                     c. Cassa or Tamburo   - Italian

CYMBAL

1. It is an untuned instrument.

2. It is a pair of round plates made up of brass alloy.

3. The cymbal can be played in various ways:
   a. A single cymbal can be suspended from a frame and be struck with a stick.
       (To produce a roll, two sticks are used)
   b. It can be brought together in a brushing, sliding manner.

4. a. To allow the sound to continue vibrating till it dies away naturally, the term 'laissez vibrer' is used.
   b. To damp the sound at once, the plates are held to the player's side and the term 'sec' is used.

5. Foreign name for the cymbal: a. Becken   - German
                                 b. Cymbales   - French
                                 c. Piatti or Cinelli - Italian

GONG

1. It is an untuned instrument.

2. It is similarly shaped as the cymbal but is heavier with a deeper rim.

3. It is capable of producing a gradual rippling crescendo when struck in a quiet repeated manner.

4. Foreign name for the gong: Tam-tam - German, French and Italian.

TRIANGLE

1. It is an untuned instrument.

2. It is a steel rod bent into the shape of a triangle and is left open at one corner.

3. A roll can be played on the triangle by moving the rod rapidly back and forth inside the angle.

4. It is capable of producing a high, bell-like and penetrating sound.

5. Foreign name for the triangle:
   a. Triangel - German
   b. Triangle - French
   c. Triangolo - Italian

TAMBOURINE

1. It is an untuned instrument.

2. It is a small single-skinned drum with jingles like tiny cymbals slotted in the narrow shell.

3. There are various ways of playing the tambourine:
   a. Striking it with the right hand knuckles, finger tips or fist, or tapping it against the knee.
   b. It can be shaken in the air to produce the *'jingle roll'.
   c. It can be placed on the player's lap and rolled with sticks or fingers with the strokes made near the rim.
   d. By running a moistened thumb round the rim of the tambourine to produce a *'jingle roll'.
   These two 'jingle roll' can be differentiated by using the terms 'shake' or 'thumb'.

4. Foreign name for the tambourine:
   a. Schellentrommel or Tamburin - German
   b. Tambour de Basque - French
   c. Tamburo basco or Tamburino - Italian

CASTANET

1. It is an untuned instrument.

2. It is a Spanish instrument consisting of a pair of small wooden shells. They are clicked together between the thumb and the forefinger.

3. Foreign name for the castanet:
   a. Kastagnetten - German
   b. Castagnettes - French
   c. Castagnette - Italian

THE WOODEN BLOCK

1. It is an untuned instrument.

2. It is an oblong piece of wood which is struck with a wooden mallet to produce a hard 'tok-tok' sound.

MARACAS

1. It is an untuned instrument.

2. It is a pair of gourds containing dry seeds and are shaken like a rattle.

BONGOS

1. It is an untuned instrument.

2. It originated from Cuba and is a pair of small single-headed drums.
   They are joined together horizontally and is played with the bare hands.

SLEIGH BELLS

1. It is an untuned instrument.

2. These are round hollow metal bells, each with a loose metal ball inside and are shaken by hand.

3. Foreign name for the sleigh bell: a. Schellen - German
                                                      b. Grelots   - French
                                                      c. Sonagli - Italian

WHIP

1. It is an untuned instrument.

2. These are two flat pieces of wood which are hinged together.
   The crack of a whip is imitated when they are clapped together.

3. Foreign name for the whip: a. Fouet   - French
                                              b. Frusta - Italian

Performance Direction

1. Muta D in C   -   Change tuning from D to C.

2. Laissez Vibrer   -   Cymbals are allowed to vibrate until the sound dies away naturally.

3. Sec   -   Damp the sound of the cymbal at once.

4. Roll   -   Rapidly alternating the blows from the two drum-sticks to create a sustained sound.

Symbol: *tr*   OR

Score Reading

1. The percussion instruments are placed between the brass and the stringed instruments.
    As the member of this section varies from work to work, the arrangement of the instruments
    are in no particular order.

2. The percussion instruments are used to emphasize a certain musical effect.
    Its main functions are to:
    a. Add variety to tone colour (e.g.: cymbals, triangle)
    b. Create special rhythmic effect (e.g.: bass drum, timpani)
    c. Create special melodic effect (e.g.: harp, xylophone)

Foreign Terms For The Orchestral Instruments

FAMILY	ENGLISH	FRENCH	ITALIAN	GERMAN
Percussion	Kettledrum (K.D.)	Timbales (timb.)	Timpani (timp.)	Pauken (pk.)
	Triangle (trgl., tri.)	Triangle (trgl.)	Triangolo (trg.)	Triangel (trg., trigl.)
	Bass drum (B.D.)	Grosse caisse (G.C., Gr.C.)	Gran cassa (G.C., Gr.C.)	Gross trommel (Gr.Tr.)
	Snare drum or Side drum (S.D.)	Tambour (tamb.) or Caisse claire (c.cl.)	Tamburo piccolo (t.picc., tb.p.) or Tamburo militare (t.m., t.mil.)	Kleine trommel (Kl.Tr.)
	Tenor drum (T.D.)	Caisse roulante (c.roul)	Cassa rulante (c.rul.)	Rührtrommel (rührtr.)
	Tambourine (tamb.)	Tambour de Basque (T. de B.)	Tamburo basco or Tamburino (tb.b., tamb.)	Tamburin or Schellentrommel (tambr.)
	Tubular bells (T.B.)	Cloches	Campane or Campanelle (camp.)	Glocken (glck.)
	Gong	Tam-tam (t.t., tamt.)	Tam-tam	Tam-tam (t.t.)
	Castanets (cast.)	Castagnette	Castagnette	Kastagnetten
	Glockenspiel (Glock.)	Carillon (car.)	Campanette or Campanelli (cmpli.)	Glockenspiel (glcksp., glsp)
	Xylophone (xyl.)	Xylophone (xylo., xylop.)	Silofono or Xilofono (xil.)	Xylophone (xylo.)
	Vibraphone	Vibraphone	Vibratono	Vibraphone
	Celesta (cel.)	Céleste or Célesta (cél.)	Celesta (cel.)	Celesta (cel.)
	Cymbal (cym.)	Cymbales (cymb.)	Piatti (P., Piat., Ptti.)	Becken (bck., beck.)

6. THE HARP

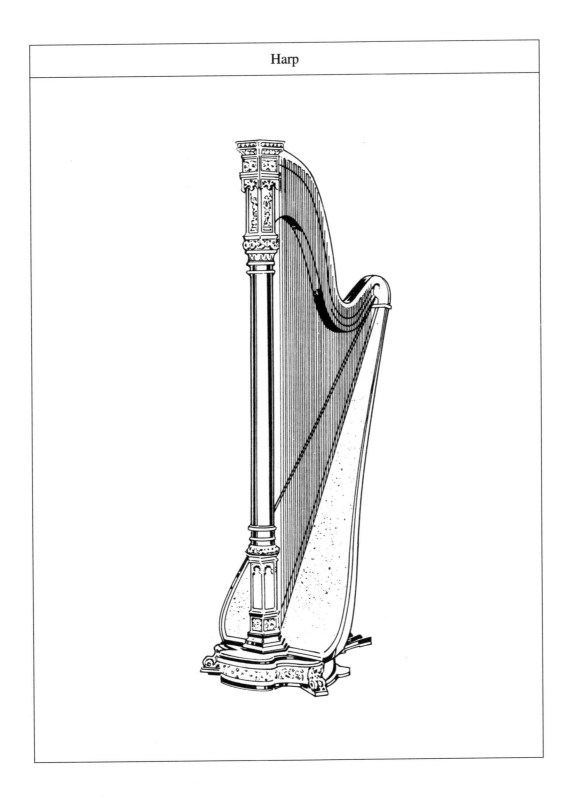

Harp

General Information

1. The harp does not belong to any specific family.

2. Its part is written on two staves in the treble and bass clef (like the piano part).
   It has 47 strings and 7 pedals.

3. The harp is tuned in the key of C flat major.

4. The harpist is seated with the harp resting on the right shoulder. The strings are plucked with the thumb and the first three fingers of both hands, one on each side of the instrument.

5. The modern harp was developed in the early 19th century by Erard.

6. It is capable of playing the *arpeggio* chords and *glissando* very effectively.

   a. **Arpeggio**

   i. Harfen

   ii. Harfen

   iii. Harp

   Britten's "The Young Person's Guide To The Orchestra"

b. **Glissando**

i.   1re Harpe

Rimsky-Korsakov's
Scheherazade (4th movement)

ii.   Arpa

7. Harmonics can also be produced on the harp.

    a. It is obtained in the same manner as the stringed instruments by lightly touching a
       certain point along the length of the string while plucking it.

    b. The sound produced is an octave higher than the 'open' string note.

8. The tone produced by the harp is not strong and this limits its use in the orchestra.
    When used, it is to give special musical effects such as delicate and graceful sound.

9. Each of the seven pedals controls all the notes with the same letter-name.
    E.g.: one for all the 'C's, one for all the 'D's, etc.
    There are three notches on which the pedal can rest on to produce a '♯', a '♭' or a '♮' note
    so that a complete chromatic scale can be obtained.

10. Two harps are commonly used in the standard symphony orchestra. However, the number of harps
    used may vary according to the requirements of a musical work.

11. Foreign name for the harp: a. Harfe   -   German

                                     b. Harpe   -   French

                                     c. Arpa   -   Italian

Performance Direction

1. Pres de la table   -   Plucking the strings near the soundboard.

2. Bisbigliando   -   Playing the repeated notes quickly and softly by using the fingers of both hands.

3. Sons etouffes   -   The string is damped to produce a staccato sound.

4. ⌀   -   Harmonic - the sound produced will sound an octave higher than written.

5. Glissando   -   Drawing the fingers rapidly across the strings of a harp.

Range of notes for the harp

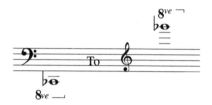

7. THE KEYBOARD INSTRUMENTS

Piano	Clavichord
Harpsichord	**Pipe organ**

The Instruments

PIANO

1. The piano was invented towards the end of the 17th century by Bartolomeo Cristofori.

2. It only gained popularity in the classical period and gradually replaced the harpsichord as the favourite keyboard media.

3. There are 88 keys on the modern piano. The high-pitched notes are to the player's right and the low-pitched notes are to the left.

4. The tone on the piano is produced by hammers hitting at the strings when a key is depressed. A damper stops the string from vibrating further when the key is released.

5. There are three pedals on the piano:
   a. The left 'soft' pedal or the 'una corda' pedal softens the tone produced when depressed. To release the left pedal, the term 'tre corde' is used.
   b. The middle 'sostenuto' pedal sustains selected notes when depressed.
   c. The right 'sustaining' pedal or 'damper' pedal lifts the dampers off the strings when it is depressed to sustain the notes and to enrich the tone produced.

Symbol
i.   Ped.
ii.   Ped. ———⌐
iii. Ped.   *

These mean : depress the right (sustaining) pedal, then release it.

6. The piano is seldom used in the orchestra. When used, it is as the soloist of a piano concerto with orchestral accompaniment.

7. Foreign name for the piano:
   a. Klavier   - German
   b. Piano   - French
   c. *Pianoforte - Italian

   *The word 'pianoforte' literally means soft-loud.

CLAVICHORD

1. The clavichord is a small keyboard instrument with a compass of about four octaves.

2. It has no pedals.

3. The tone on the clavichord is produced by metal tangent hitting at the string when a key is depressed.

4. It is used as a solo keyboard instrument from the 15th century to the 18th century.

5. The clavichord is capable of producing soft and delicate sound.

6. A type of vibrato 'Bebung', can be obtained by vibrating a depressed key.

7. The clavichord was mainly confined to domestic use because of its soft tone production. However, in the 20th century, the clavichord was revived for old music.

HARPSICHORD

1. The harpsichord was the favourite keyboard media in the Baroque.

2. The tone on the harpsichord is produced by quills plucking at the strings when a key is depressed. There are two or more strings to each note.

3. The range of dynamic is narrow for the harpsichord. It is not capable of producing very loud or very soft tone.

4. The harpsichord usually has two keyboards, sometimes even three.

5. The harpsichord has very little sustaining power, that is why ornaments are often used in Baroque music to emphasize a note.

6. The harpsichord uses pedals to control the quality of tone by selecting the type of quills used to pluck the strings.

7. Foreign name for the harpsichord:
   a. Cembalo   - German
   b. Clavecin   - French
   c. Cembalo or Clavicembalo - Italian

PIPE ORGAN

1. The Organ has
   a. a pedal board (played by the feet) called Pedal Organ.
   b. two to five manual keyboards (played by the hands).
   The names of the manuals are as follow:
       i.   First manual   :   Great Organ
       ii. Second manual :   Swell Organ
       iii. Third manual   :   Choir Organ
       iv. Fourth manual :   Solo Organ
       v.   Fifth manual   :   Echo Organ

2. There are two main kinds of stop on the organ:
   a. Flue stop
   b. Reed stop (for high-pitched notes)

3. Other common stops that were used are the
   a. Diapason stop
   b. Mutation stop
   c. Mixture stop
   d. Bourbon stop

4. Combination of different stops on different keyboards produce varied tone.

5. The tone on the organ is produced by wind blowing through a series of pipes which is connected to a keyboard.

MODERN ELECTRIC ORGAN

1. It does not use any pipes.

2. The sound is produced when a set of metallic plates is activated by electricity.

8. CHAMBER MUSIC

General Information

1. Chamber music is a piece of vocal or instrumental music written for a combined group of solo players to be performed in a small room. Each player has a part.

2. Chamber music is known by the number of players in the group:

	Number of Players
Duet	2
Trio	3
Quartet	4
Quintet	5
Sextet	6
Septet	7
Octet	8

3. The following are some generally used chamber combinations:

Duet	Violin and Piano
	Cello and Piano
	Clarinet and Piano
String Trio	Violin, Viola, Cello
Piano Trio	Piano, Violin, Cello
String Quartet	2 Violins, Viola, Cello (ie. violin and string trio)
Piano Quartet	Piano, Violin, Viola, Cello (ie. piano and string trio)
Flute Quartet	Flute, Violin, Viola, Cello (ie. flute and string trio)
Vocal Quartet (Mixed Voice Quartet)	Soprano, Alto, Tenor, Bass
String Quintet	2 Violins, 2 Violas, Cello **OR** 2 Violins, Viola, 2 Cellos
Piano Quintet	Piano, 2 Violins, Viola, Cello (ie. piano and string quartet)
Clarinet Quintet	Clarinet, 2 Violins, Viola, Cello (ie. clarinet and string quartet)
Horn Quintet	Horn and string quartet
Wind Quintet	Flute, Oboe, Clarinet, French horn, Bassoon
Vocal Quintet	2 Sopranos, Contralto, Tenor, Bass **OR** Soprano, Contralto, 2 Tenors, Bass
String Sextet	2 Violins, 2 Violas, 2 Cellos
Septet	Violin, Viola, Cello, Double bass, Clarinet, Bassoon, Horn
String Octet	4 Violins, 2 Violas, 2 Cellos **OR** 2 Violins, Viola, Cello, Double bass, Clarinet, Bassoon, Horn

Chamber Musical Scores

Example I:

This is a musical score of a duet between the clarinet and the piano.

Example II:

This is a musical score of a string trio.

Example III:

Mozart's
Oboe Quartet in F, K370

This is a musical score of an oboe quartet.

Example IV:

Mozart's
Clarinet Quintet, K581 (2nd movement)

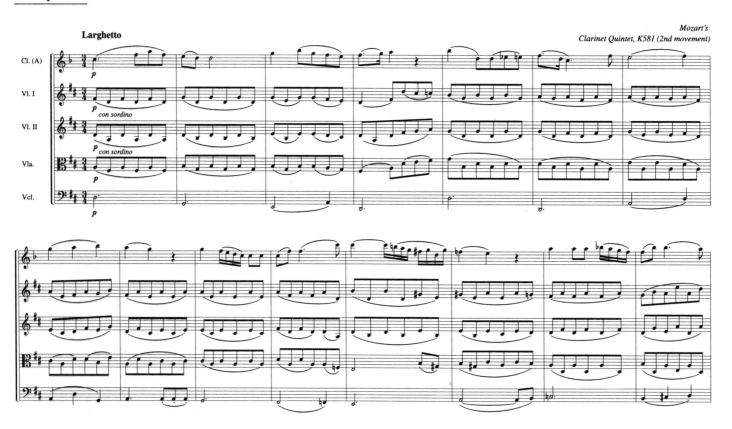

This is a musical score of a clarinet quintet.

70

9. ORCHESTRATION

General Information

1. The symphony orchestra is made up of the four instrumental families:

    a. Woodwind   b. Brass   c. Percussion   d. String

2. The four families appear in the following *downward order* in the orchestral full score.

WOODWIND	Piccolo Flute Oboe Cor anglais Clarinet Bass clarinet Bassoon Double bassoon
BRASS	Horn Trumpet Trombone Tuba
PERCUSSION	Timpani Other percussion instruments
STRING	Violin Viola Cello Double bass

3. The **harp** is placed **between the percussion** and **the string family.**

4. The voice parts (chorus) or a solo instrument in a concerto is placed above the string family.

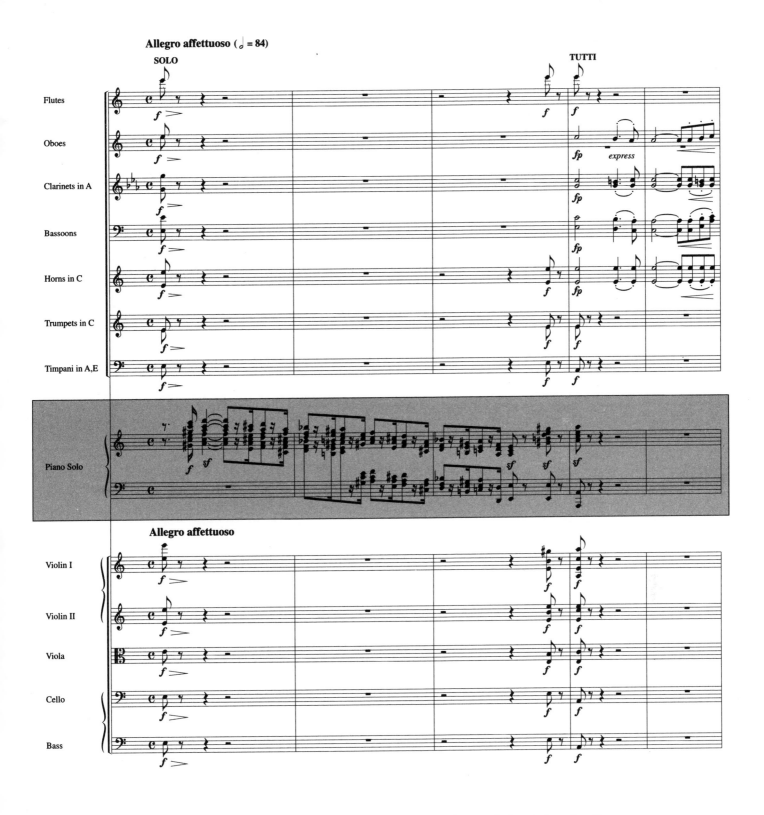

The **soloist of a concerto** is placed **between the percussion** and **the string family.**

The **chorus part** is placed **above the string family.**

In *older scores, the chorus part is placed between the viola and the cello stave, thus dividing the string score into two.

*This arrangement, though commonly used then, was not only confined to older scores.
It was also sometimes used by some later composers, like Brahms in his Requiem.

75

5. The number of players in an orchestra varies, though the standard orchestra commonly has about 80 players.

6. The number of each instrument used depends on its ability to produce loud or soft tonal volume.

Tchaikovsky's Symphony

The brass instruments are capable of producing a very loud tone, therefore, to balance the 'f' played by the strings, the brass instruments need to play only at a 'mf' level.

Performance Direction

1. a2 or zu2   -

    a. For the string instruments, it is an instruction to the players to divide into two groups, each playing one note.

    b. For other orchestral instruments, (i.e., flute, horn), it is an instruction to the players to play the same note or notes in unison.
    (a3 refers to three players, a4 refers to four players)

2. Colla Parte   -   Follow the soloist or singer.
   (Colla Voce)

3. Con Pedal   -   Depress the sustaining pedal.
   (Con Ped.)

4. Divisi   -   To divide into two or more groups.
   (Div.)   (e.g.: 'Divisi a3' means divide into three groups.)

5. Senza Pedal   -   Do not use the sustaining pedal.
   (Senza Ped.)

6. Tacet   -   Complete silence in the orchestra.

7. Tre Corde   -   Release the soft pedal of the piano.

8. Tutti   -   A passage where the whole orchestra (or a section of it) plays together after a solo passage.

9. Una Corda   -   Depress the soft pedal of the piano.

10. Unisono   -   All performers play the same note after a 'divisi' passage.
   (Unis.)

Foreign Term	Meaning
Con Sordini (Italian) Mit Dampfer (German) Avec Sourd (French)	with a mute
Senza Sordini (Italian) Ohne Dampfer (German) Otez les Sourds (French)	without a mute

THE SITTING ARRANGEMENT OF THE ORCHESTRA

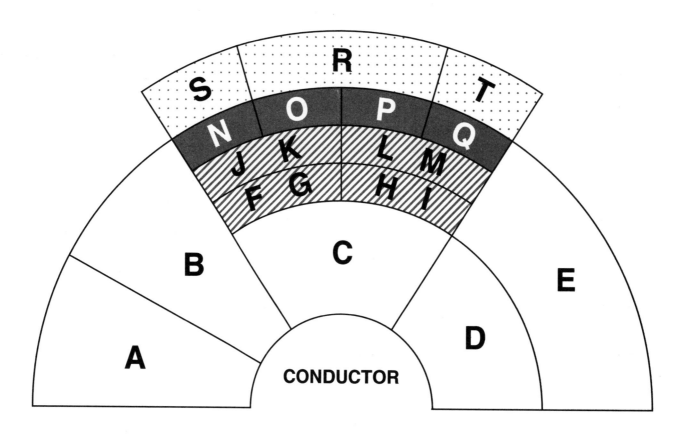

STRING FAMILY ▢		WOODWIND FAMILY ▨	
A - First Violin		**F** - Piccolo	
B - Second violin		**G** - Flute	
C - Viola		**H** - Oboe	
D - Violoncello		**I** - Cor anglais	
E - Double Bass		**J** - Clarinet	
		K - Saxophone	
		L - Bassoon	
		M - Double Bassoon	

BRASS FAMILY ▇		PERCUSSION FAMILY ⠿	
N - Horn		**S** - Harp	
O - Trumpet		**R** - Other percussion instruments	
P - Trombone		**T** - Timpani	
Q - Tuba			

10. DEVELOPMENT OF THE ORCHESTRA

The Baroque

The Woodwind Family

1. The woodwind instruments played a passive role in the baroque music and is seldom used.

2. When used
   a. The oboe would generally imitate the violin part.
   b. The flute would generally imitate the trumpet part.

The Brass Family

1. The brass instruments were seldom used in the Baroque music.

2. When used
   a. The trumpet is generally paired off with the timpani.
   b. The trumpet would imitate the flute.

3. *'Clarino playing'* in trumpet is a much used technique.
   This is the playing of notes in the very high register.
   It is very difficult and requires much skill.

The Percussion Family

In the Baroque, the timpani were often used together with the trumpets.

The String Family

1. In the Baroque and even early classical music,
   a. The first and second violin generally plays in unison or in thirds.
   b. The viola usually doubles the cello part, playing the same notes.
      However, the first and second violins sometimes play different melodies to create melodic interest.

2. The double bass was generally used only in very large works like oratorio, opera, concerto grosso, etc.

3. Up till the classical period, only four staves were used for the string score, with the cello and the double bass sharing a stave.

Baroque Musical Scores

Example I:

Arne

A • When used, the oboe would generally imitate the violin part.

B • The presence of figured bass is a characteristic feature of Baroque music.

C • The first and second violins generally play in unison or in thirds.

Example II:

SICILIANA

Largo

Handel
Oboe Concerto in B flat

A • The first and second violins playing in thirds.

B • The first and second violins playing different melodies to create melodic interest.

C • The presence of figured bass is a characteristic feature of Baroque music.

82

The Classical

The Woodwind Family

1. Haydn or Mozart usually used only one flute for their works.
   It was Beethoven who introduced the double woodwind (i.e. 2 flutes, 2 oboes, 2 clarinets, 2 bassoons) and since then, two flutes were commonly used.

2. Mozart established the use of the clarinet in the symphony orchestra.

3. In general, the role of the woodwind was rather passive in the classical works.
   It was usually used to double the first violin part and to help create louder volume in loud passages.

The Brass Family

1. Beethoven increased the number of horns used from two to four.

2. Beethoven also established the use of trombones in the orchestra.

3. Due to the limitation of notes in the harmonic series (crooks were then used),
   the brass instruments were commonly used to accompany and
   to give tonal support in loud passages.

The Percussion Family

1. The timpani were the only standard member of the percussion family.

2. The timpani were always used in pairs and were tuned to the tonic and dominant of a scale.

The String Family

1. The double bass became a standard member of the orchestra from the classical period onwards.

2. For most works written before 1800, the cello part is doubled by the double bass. As the double bass transposes an octave lower than written, its part will sound an octave lower than the cello although both are written on the same stave.

3. Beethoven introduced the use of five staves for the string score by separating the cello from the double bass, giving each a stave of its own.

4. However, some music after the time of Beethoven still use four staves for the string score, especially when the cello and the double bass are playing the same notes.

Classical Musical Scores

Example I:

Haydn's
Symphony no.2, op.30

A • The oboes are doubling the first violin parts and also helping to create a louder volume in the '*f*' passages.

B • Four staves are used for the string score.

C • 'a2' means : the two bassoons play in unison.

Example II:

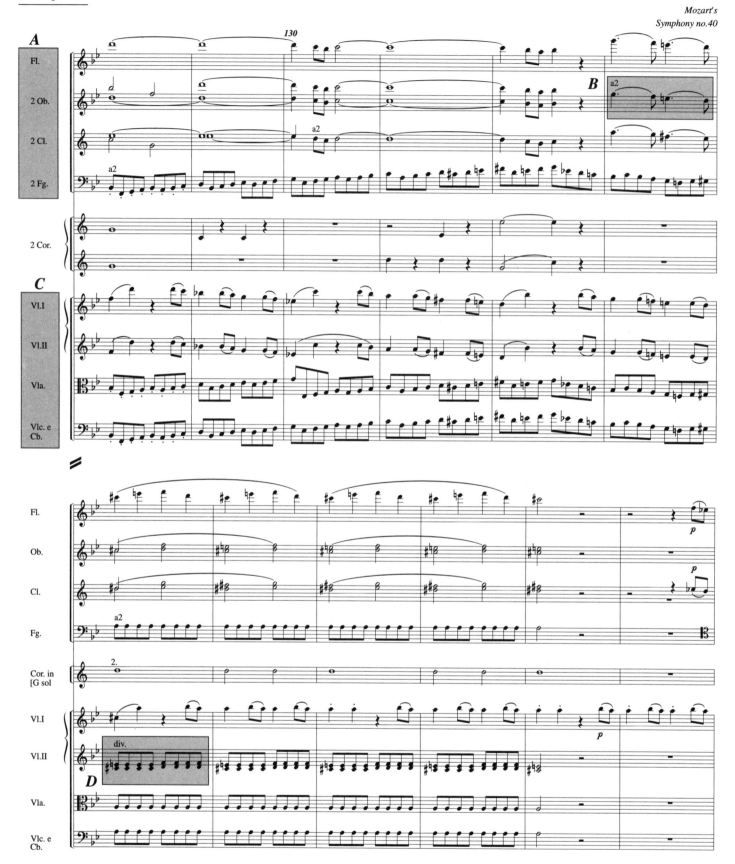

A • 1 flute, 2 oboes, 2 clarinets, 2 bassoons are used in the woodwind section.

B • 'a2' means : the two oboes play in unison.

C • Four staves are used for the string score.

D • 'Div.' refers to the second violin group dividing into 2 groups, each taking a part.

The Romantic

The Woodwind Family

1. The woodwind section was expanded to balance with the larger string section.

2. New additional instruments were added
   a. *Piccolo   b. *Double bassoon   c. Cor anglais   d. Bass clarinet
   Beethoven was responsible for these additions.
   Note that Beethoven's life spanned from the late Classical into the early Romantic.

3. Wagner introduced the use of triple woodwind (i.e. 3 flutes, 3 oboes, 3 clarinets, 3 bassoons).

4. The woodwind instruments were given more melodious and solo parts to play.
   They are no longer confined to the role of doubling the string parts.

The Brass Family

1. With the invention of the valves (piston) in the early 19th century, a much wider scope of notes can be obtained by the brass instruments.

2. As such, more melodic and even solo parts were given to the brass instruments.

The Percussion Family

1. From the Romantic onwards, the percussion section was expanded by the many new additionals.

2. The timpani were the only percussion instrument that can be considered as a standard member of the orchestra.

3. Other commonly used additional percussion instruments were bass drum, cymbal, side drum and triangle.

4. From time to time, a wide variety of percussion instruments were used depending on the requirement of the piece.
   They were termed as the temporary instruments without taking any permanent place in the orchestra.
   These instruments were celesta, xylophone, bells, gongs, etc.

The String Family

1. From the classical period to the twentieth century, there are no additional new instruments in the string family.

2. The only notable difference is that the string section expanded in size.

3. From the Romantic onwards, many playing techniques such as col legno, pizzicato, etc., were used to create special musical effects.

Romantic Musical Scores

Example I:

A • The woodwind parts are more melodious and no longer confined to the role of accompanying.

B • Although this is a Romantic work, the string score is still written in 4 staves because both the cello and the double bass are playing the same notes.

C • A wider range of dynamic is used.

Example II:

Extract I

Mendelssohn
A Midsummer Night's Dream

Extract II

The two extracts above are taken from *different parts* of a *same piece* of work. Note that the composers after the time of Beethoven have a choice of using either four or five staves for the string score. If the cello and the double bass are playing the same notes, four staves will be used for the strings. However, if the cello and the double bass are playing different notes, five staves will then be used for the strings.

Example III:

A • 3 flutes and 4 horns are used. This indicates a piece from the Romantic period *onwards*.

B • The range of dynamic is wide and dramatic.

C • This means 'Strike with the drumstick'.

D • The first and second trombone share the tenor clef while the third trombone shares a stave with the bass tuba using the bass clef.

The Twentieth Century

From the late Romantic onwards, there were no fixed number as to the woodwind, brass, string and percussion instruments used. The number of instruments used depend on the requirement of a piece. Sometimes, only selected members of a family is used.

Twentieth Century Musical Scores

Example I:

Aaron Copland's
Variations on a Shaker Melody

A • From the Romantic period onwards, the woodwind are given more solo parts to play.

B • This is the symbol for 'harmonics' (𝅗𝅥).

C • From the late Romantic period onwards, only selected members of the string family are sometimes used in certain works.

Example II:

Britten's
War Requiem

A • Rhythm plays an important role in the 20th century music.
Time-signatures sometimes change in every bar or so.

B • These (♩) means that the note has to be stopped.

C • A key-signature is used in the horn part. It was only in the 20th century that this idea was introduced.

93

TABLE

Summary On The Comparison Between The **Instrumentation** Of Different Stylistic Eras.

	BAROQUE (1600-1750)	CLASSICAL (1750-1820)	ROMANTIC (19th century)
	• 17th century • Early 18th century • 1st half of the 18th century	• Late 18th century • 2nd half of the 18th century • Early 19th century	
STRING	• Violin • Viola • Cello • Double bass - rarely used	• Violin • Viola • Cello • Double bass	• Violin • Viola • Cello • Double bass
WOODWIND	• Oboe • Bassoon • Flute (transverse)	• 1 or 2 flutes • 2 oboes • 2 bassoons • 2 clarinets	• Flute • Oboe • Clarinet • Bassoon • Piccolo • Bass clarinet • English horn • Double bassoon
BRASS	• Horn • Trumpet • Trombone	• 2 horns • 2 trumpets • Trombone (less popular)	• 4 horns • 2 trumpets • 3 trombones (2 tenor, 1 bass) • Tuba
PERCUSSION	• Timpani (only when neccesary)	• Timpani (in pairs)	• 3 timpani **Many additionals:** • Bass drum • Side drum • Harp • Triangle • Gong • Castanet • Cymbal • Celesta, etc.

All instruments are written in the order of their positions in the orchestral score.

About the author

Lee Ching Ching was born on the 1st of January. She was, upon recommendation approved as a Fellow of the Trinity College of London in pianoforte performance in 1988. Six months later, she was entitled the professional qualification in music education.

Since then, she has been lecturing and specialising in the teaching of musical subjects at diploma level. Among her achievements are producing students who have done her proud by winning musical awards at international level for outstanding performance as well as winning scholarships to colleges overseas.

Currently lecturing at the Mara Institute of Technology (ITM), she is making financial contributions, based on the royalties of this book, for charitable causes.